Ebony Verses

Fatima Sacoh

BookLeaf Publishing

India | USA | UK

Presentation by *BookLeaf Publishing*

Web: www.bookleafpub.com

E-mail: info@bookleafpub.com

ISBN: 9789360945473

First edition 2024

Dedicated To My Mother,

Who deserves grace for doing the best that she could.

ACKNOWLEDGEMENT

First I want to give a big thanks to my friend, Joyce Hounkarin, for encouraging me to release this book and always seeing the talent and greatness that I sometimes can't see in myself. Unfortunately, I can go through times when I don't understand what my purpose is and don't celebrate the accomplishments that I have been able to achieve despite where I come from and where I was told that I was supposed to end up. Thank you for always reminding me that I am far from mediocre and that I can have the world if I just go on and chase it.

A special thanks to my creative writing teachers at Bronx Academy of Letters, Samantha Thornhill and Elana Bell, who saved my life by introducing me to the power of writing. Although I had been writing since I was 11 years old, it was something that I would do when I had to for school, and while many of my teachers in middle school complimented me on my writing, it was these ladies who not only taught me the different ways that I can incorporate my repressed emotions in my writing but encouraged me to share that vulnerability with the world and unconsciously, touch the lives of other people going through the same issues.

My best friends, Muslimah and Monaya, are not only my always does to be my practice audiences, but I am always my biggest cheerleader. Thank you guys for always being there for me during my highs and my lows. During my beautiful moments and my ugly moments. During the times when I am well put together and when I am all over the place. I am used to always having to put on the mask of "perfection" in fear of losing people in my life. Thank you for seeing the beauty in me in all facets and loving me unconditionally. Thank you for showing for helping me make it through the darkness through true friendship.

Lastly, Thank you to every person who is reading this book right now. Sharing art, especially personal art, is scary and opens up a world full of judgment and disappointment. Thank you for being open to following my journey. There are a thousand poetry books out there; Thank you for taking the time to read this one. I have nothing but love for every one of ya'll.

Black Orchid

A young black queen with strength unmeasured,
A heart seeking love, not just for pleasure,
She gives without asking for anything back,
Yet society reduces her worth to an ass clap.

A black girl disrespected by her supposed
brother,
Called "hoe" and "bitch," unlike any other,
To be a black girl is to face media disdain,
For lips, ass, breasts, curves - yet praise for
others' gain.

To be a black girl is to carry a legacy of pain,
From Sarah Bartmaan to modern-day's cruel
refrain,
Judged by the shade, the tightness of jeans,
The texture of hair, the brands she leans.

Divided by relationships and trivialities,
Reality TV showcases our disparities,
Like a subtle genocide, killing our pride,
Can we regain what we feel inside?

Can a caged bird learn to fly,
When its wings have been clipped, oh, so high?

Can sistas reclaim their queenship,
Even with souls cracked, wounded by the whip?

Little black girl, rise above the noise,
Let go of comparisons, find your own voice,
Hair snatching, eyes scratching, televised,
But within you, strength that can't be disguised.

Can we break free from this societal trap?
Reclaim our worth, bridge the gap?
Little black girl, becomes a Black Woman,
Embrace the spirits of Nefertiti, Nzinga, and
then some.

Strong and driven, labeled "Angry Black
Woman,"
When silence is refused, and they turn to
violence, man,
R.I.P Sandra Bland, your name a rallying cry,
For the black women who refuse to stand by.

Being black is a sentence, a truth we've known,
Yet within our community, we're often left alone.
But in that solitude, a strength will rise,
As black women, reclaiming our prize.

Ode To My Dark Skin

They say the blacker the berry,
The sweeter the juice,
A cliché, perhaps, but it holds the truth.
There were times I despised you,
Debated your worth,
Ashamed of your hue,
As if it were a curse.
Mainstream media, a wolf in sheep's clothing,
Sells fair skin as a golden ticket, so loathing
I was of you, my skin, my identity,
I sought to change you,
Lost in my vanity.

I abused you with creams, blinded by the lie,
Your true beauty hidden, brings tears to my eyes.
Could you forgive me, for the shame I brought?
For the words of color-struck fools,
The battles I fought?

You are the symbol of strength,
Queen Nefertiti reborn,
Your blackness wraps around me,
My freakum dress is worn.
You elevate my game,
Make me turn my back on the lames,

Look who's now ego trippin',
And you're the one to acclaim.

Draped in the richness of melted Godiva,
Sweet chocolate,
I'm on fire.
No, I'm not cocky, I'm confident,
Laughing at those who say you shouldn't be
desired.

How dare they associate you with ugliness,
Their ignorance,
it seems, is quite contagious.
What you're made with, can't be debated,
You're closer to gold,
And that can't be tainted.

Never leave me alone,
Keep blessing me with your kisses,
For the blacker the berry, the sweeter the juice,
And you are what I was blessed with.

Inner City Blues

NYPD is ready to keep your souls in check,
Weed and piss the aura in the project stairsteps,
Inhale cuz we're in hell,
Guns blast no one tells,
Snitches receive bulletholes,
Street gangs are in control.

Leaking ceiling,
Little dreaming,
Series of nightmares but who the hell cares?
It's like a third-world country that the
government pushes aside,
The ghetto is dying but no one hears the cries,
9-year-old boys selling white rocks,
Little girls doing anything to be on top,
There are no children in the hood,
Innocence doesn't exist yet it's still all good,
Do you know how it feels to be raised with fear?
Death might come today but you can't shed a
tear,
I never ran from the Ku Klux Klan,
Yet I'm running from a black man,
And this ain't to bash my brother's,
I just want to feel protected.

I got the inner city blues like Marvin,
Trigger-happy cops looking for a target,
If you don't agree then what news station are you
watching,
Cuz bodies are being dropped from NYC to
Compton,
I ain't complaining when I'm stating the blues,
Just coming from the heart and speaking the
truth,
This ain't a story or some goddamn fantasy,
Just the inner city blues you gotta live through to
believe.

I Wish

I wish I could say that I love you,
I wish that I can say I want to stay in your arms
forever,
I wish I could say that you make my heart beat
faster and slower every time I see you,
I wish that I could say I want to follow you
wherever.

If loving someone was so easy,
You will be my first contender,
But I can't have a love full of lies,
You don't deserve a pretender.

I wish that I can say my face glows when you
enter,
That you are the only man I want to belong to,
I wish that I could say you make my heart
surrender,
That the feelings I have for you are true.

You deserve to be with a women who get
butterflies when you cross her mind,
Who finds your soft kisses so sweet,
Who will climb mountains and cross the seas for
you,
I'm just so sorry that woman isn't me.

Trap Queen

Together we stand, in riches or ruin,
From the start, your secrets I've been stewing.
I'm your shield, your partner in crime,
Through the hardest times, I promise to climb.

With courage in my heart and steel by my side,
On the battlefield, I will not hide.
Bursting through barriers, a force untamed,
I'm your queen, in this wild game.
Through the city we ride, our anthem blaring,
"Us Against the World", our souls declared.
I may not smoke, but I'll take a hit,
For this wild love, I admit, I'm unfit.

Imagine a day without your saving grace,
A world without your familiar face.
For you, I'd risk it all, no hesitation,
Never betraying our sacred relation.

They say love can make you lose your mind,
But with you, true strength I find.
All I need is courage and a shield,
With you, we'll conquer every field.

We'll seize the world, claim diamonds and
pearls,
In this whirlwind life, as it unfurls.
And when it ends, let me rest on your heart,
No tears, no regrets, just a new start.
For I lived and died a warrior, true,
A life of lessons, learned from you.

Sometimes I Cry

Sometimes I cry,
But few will ever know,
My smile is a disguise when I'm feeling low.

Tears cascade down my cheeks,
Relentless like a fall,
Hidden sorrows I keep,
Behind a laughter wall.

Sometimes I cry,
My pain you can't envision,
For in this world of hurt,
There's little empathy with compassion.

Sadness turns to anger,
Apathy becomes the norm,
Numbness to the chaos,
An everyday performance.

Life's a play with no rehearsal,
Waiting for my Tony's call,
Acting is my survival,
to navigate stress and all.

Walk in my shoes,

And grasp my soulful blues,
Lonely nights I've cried,
Cleansing with hopes to renew.

Haunted by dark thoughts,
But death holds no fright,
For what's beyond can't match the despair of my
reality's kite.

Sometimes I cry,
As teardrops freely fall,
Standing tall becomes a strain,
When all I want is to sprawl.

Blood Diamonds

My eyes gleam like diamonds on my necklace,
Diamonds on my wrist,
Got these niggas acting reckless,
Blood diamonds,
Like crimson claws,
Have snatched my father's brethren,
Colonization,
a thief,
Stole my continent's rich inheritance,
Diamonds, they're part of my lineage,
Yet I'm missing part of my heritage,
Diamonds, a harsh beauty, cut from the
elements,
With a dark history, its shadow is still prevalent,
Wars from Sierra Leone to Baltimore's streets,
Diamonds bling, a cruel symphony to the sound
of gunshots' beats.

They speak of the diamond in the rough,
And I have met many, their edges tough,
Diamonds mean well,
But the complexities they contain,
Diamonds, like a lover's whisper,
Bring fleeting pleasure, but also pain.

So next time you're rockin' your diamonds, so
bright,
Remember it's at the expense of another's plight.

Tomorrow

If today feels like the end for you,
And that sickening voice in your head that tells
you that a permanent sleep should ensue,
Please remember tomorrow,
The tomorrow that will be closer to better days,
The tomorrow that will be closer to all your pain
washing away,
The tomorrow where you can finally understand
that hard times are temporary,
The tomorrow that will have you be a step closer
to your dream,
The Tomorrow where you have the chance to
gain even more wisdom,
Tomorrow when staying with us is the right
decision,
Please just wait till tomorrow,
And if tomorrow does not get better then wait
till the next day,
And if the next day is not doing it for you then
please hold on till the next day,
Please wait,
Wait till that strong feeling is bored and no
longer wants to stay,
Because emotions are strong yet fickle,
They are like rocks on the beach,

One strong wave and you realize how one
impact can be the reach,
That the troubles that you face will soon be what
you overcome,
It may be hard to see it now but you need to stay
around to witness the blessing that you will
become,
So sit down,
Take a breath,
And it's okay to reflect on all your pain and
sorrow,
Just please don't let that keep you from being
with us tomorrow.

Mama Said

Mama said don't be too easy,
Mama said don't be too fast,
Mama said to give a boy your cookie,
Then he will leave you and brag,
Mama said make sure your dress reaches to your
knees,
You don't want to look like a skank.
Make sure your make-up isn't too heavy,
Or you'll look like a tramp,
Mama said don't talk too loud,
Mama said don't be too rough,
Keep your opinions to yourself,
No man wants a woman too tough.

Mama said to learn how to cook,
You betta learn how to clean,
Make sure your man feels like a king,
And if you're lucky, he'll treat you like a queen.

Mama said to be careful with the dope boys and
the gangbangers,
Be careful with the drunks and the fiends,
They'll only bring you danger,
But when that happens make sure you scream.

But Mama didn't teach me what to do,
When your innocence is taken away,
And it wasn't the monsters from outside,
That caused your nightmares to be on replay.

Mama never taught me about cold, rough hands,
Rubbing on my smooth brown thighs,
Mama never taught me what to do,
When it's a familiar face that makes you wish
you would die,
Mama never taught me that your family could be
the ones that
harm you,
She never taught me they can be the ones that
make you scream,
She taught me to call on God when I am in
trouble,
And when I did,
He abandoned me.

Mama never taught me about the feeling,
When your reflection becomes a sight of disgust,
and even a playful gesture at the playground,
would have you trembling with a single touch,
she never taught me what to do,
when you grow up with a hatred for men,
And you can't trust even the good ones,
So you turn down every advance.

Mama taught me to play the game,
She taught me to follow the rules,
She taught me how to be a respectable, young
lady,
I just wish she would've taught me that being a
respectable, young
lady,
Does not always protect you.

Nearness Of You

Is it your voice, a melody that sets my soul
alight?
Or your smirk, a moonbeam in the darkest
night?
Does my heart dance like a hummingbird in
flight,
In the intoxicating nearness of you?

Your presence, a sunrise that paints my world
anew,
How you hold me, a fortress strong and true.
In your arms, I find a haven from life's rue,
Is it the intoxicating nearness of you?

You, my one and only, my dream in the morning
dew,
You taught me love, a language I never knew.
A stolen secret, yet my heart you've managed to
subdue,
In the agonizing nearness of you.

A twin flame ignited like a comet, beautiful but
askew,
A love that can't be, a pain only we two knew.

Yet fairness demands, this clandestine
rendezvous,
In the heartbreaking nearness of you.

I'll wait, a sentinel in the night,
For the next life's debut,
To once again experience the nearness of you.

Prayer In The Shower

In the sanctuary of solitude,
I stand,
Beneath the cascading waters,
A tranquil land.

Prayer takes flight as soap and sorrow collide,
In this sacred shower,
Where my sadness subsides.

Water dances upon my weary frame,
Cleansing not just my body,
But also my soul's pain.

Raindrops caress me,
like a gentle touch from above,
As I pour out my heart in this cathedral called
love.

In the rhythm of the water,
My prayer takes flight,
An honest confession,
hidden from human sight.

The steam embraces me,
like a comforting embrace,

Whispering secrets,
its warmth a divine grace.

With each drop that falls,
my burdens dissipate,
Carried away by the rivers of faith dilate.

God listens as the water serenades my plea,
In this sacred shower,
He hears,
He sees.

Oh,
cleansing water,
wash away my strife,
Renew my spirit,
grant me strength for life.

In this intimate space,
I find solace and power,
In my private sanctuary,
My prayer in the shower.

Whispers of Clandestine Love

In the shadows I reside, a silent guest,
A secret shared, a forbidden jest,
I wear the label that's undefined,
In the clandestine dance, where hearts invest.
Stolen moments, wrapped in veils of deceit,
A tangled web, where passions discreetly meet,
A fleeting gaze, where longing and guilt entreat,
In the clandestine whispers, love's bittersweet.

A clandestine liaison, woven in shades of gray,
Walking the tightrope, in love's intricate ballet,
Yet, I am the echo in the hushed serenade,
Caught in the tempest, where emotions may
betray.

In the moonlit tryst, where shadows conspire,
I am the secret flame, a clandestine fire,
Yet, in the heart's chambers, a quiet choir,
Singing the ballad of love's unquenchable desire.

But in this clandestine world, I'm left to ponder,
The echoes of conscience, the moral thunder,
In playing this role, I'm forced to wonder,

Can love thrive when built on secrets to
plunder?

In the quiet aftermath, where remorse takes
flight,
I bear the burden of shadows, hidden from the
light,
Yet, in this clandestine dance, I find no respite,
For love, entangled, can become a perilous
plight.

Wonder Where My Secret Lies

Many men wonder where my secret lies.
Is it the smile that blinds or the starry skies in
my eyes?
Is it the slender waist, or the curves that
surprise?
Or the high cheekbones, where elegance lies?

They question if it's the voice, soft yet firm,
Or the open mind, where ideas swarm and
churn.
Or perhaps the rhythm, in my hips that turn,
To the music's beat, in a dance unconcerned.

My secret, I say, is a confidence earned,
From years of living, lessons learned.
Told femininity was weak, its power spurned,
Surviving, not thriving, a life unadorned.

But a time came when I had to discern,
The beauty within, yearning to return.
Embracing self-love, society's concern,
A womanhood questioned, its essence firm.

My secret, you see, is not easily defined,

Many have tried but left behind.
For it's a spiritual essence, uniquely designed,
Like Moses parting the sea, a power divine.

Gambian-Yorker

In the Bronx, I was born,
Where dreams take flight,
A place full of grit,
Where the strong unite.
From Yankee Stadium's roar to graffiti-clad
walls,
I proudly stand tall,
From the Bronx, I recall.

With Gambian roots that run deep in my veins,
A heritage rich, that forever remains.
From the banks of River Gambia's flowing tide,
A proud Gambian spirit, nothing can hide.

In the streets of the Bronx,
Diversity thrives,
A melting pot of cultures,
Where hope survives.
From Grand Concourse to Soundview's
embrace,
A tapestry of stories,
A vibrant place.

The Bronx,
Where resilience meets art,

I wear this badge proudly,
Close to my heart.
And in the traditional beats of the kora's strings,
Gambian melodies,
My soul joyfully sings.

Two worlds intertwined, creating harmony,
The Bronx and Gambia is a unique symphony.
I stand as a bridge, embracing both lands,
A proud Gambian from the Bronx, that's where I
stand.

So let the Bronx ignite my fiery pride,
In Gambian traditions, I'll gracefully ride.
For the roots that shape me, can never be erased,
In the Bronx and Gambia, my heart finds its
place.

Perception

Smiling faces frozen in digital frames,
Announcements of love, life, and games,
Crafting an image, a perfect facade,
Hiding the chaos, the personal jihad.

They share their glows, their victories won,
But the battles they lose are told to none,
A curated reality, a crafted lie,
To face the truth is to defy.

Behind the screen, a world unseen,
A silent struggle, a quiet scream.
The laughter, joy, the perfect scene,
Yet, beneath it all, a different theme.

A world of hurt, of tears unshed,
Of sleepless nights and days of dread.
Yet, in the light of day, they tread,
Their silent stories are left unsaid.

In the digital realm, they wear a mask,
In their private pain, they bask.
A Herculean, unending task,
To keep it hidden, is no easy ask.

So remember well, when you scroll by,
Each post, each picture, each joyful cry,
Behind the screen, a truth may lie,
A hidden tale of the silent sky

Rockstar

In the realm of rhythm, where melodies roam,
I fell for a rockstar, a heart far from home.
His voice was a symphony, sweet and profound,
In the echoes of his music, my heart was found.

His guitar is his soulmate, his lyrics, his truth,
I was just a fan, lost in the booth.
His songs were my solace, his chords my
delight,
In the darkness of my world, he was my light.

But a rockstar's heart is a wandering tune,
It dances with the moon and sleeps till noon.
His love was a ballad, beautiful but brief,
A poignant melody, etched in grief.

He strummed my heartstrings, played me like a
song,
In his world of music, I didn't belong.
His notes were my tears, his rhythm, my pain,
In the symphony of love, I was a refrain.

His concert was over, the crowd had dispersed,
In the silence that followed, my heart was burst.
His music still lingers, his voice in my ear,

A haunting melody, I hold dear.

So, I dance to the rhythm of my broken heart,
In the music of love, playing my part.
For even in sorrow, there's a song to be sung,
In the symphony of life, we're all unsung.

Ode To My Project Queens

This is for my project queens,
For my resilient,
Hood-born dreams,
Those who've mastered the art of street smarts,
Never fooled, never tricked, playing their parts.

They scorn us for our humble address,
Yet we rise,
Earning our Masters,
Expected to be mere statistics,
But we stand firm, our resolve ballistic.

This is for my ghetto heroines,
Those who've learned to survive, to win.
Not seen as damsels in distress,
We grew up fast, in this game of chess.
They claim we lack simple class,
Good for nothing but a fleeting pass.
They try to reduce us to mere hood rats,
But we keep moving, winning, that's a fact.

This is for my inner-city bitches,
No harm meant when I use the word bitches,
The ones with the silk pressed,
Thirty Inches,

One day, we goin' all claim our riches,
We may move up, we may rise, we may
progress,
But let's never forget our roots, our address.
Our hood, our people in the trenches,
Humble beginnings, our survival benches.

So this is for my project queens,
This is for my hood-born dreams.
Never feel ashamed of where you come from,
The underdogs are always the chosen ones.

African Queen

Gently brush away those tears, my love,
Keep your head high, and don't let sorrow shove.
In your pretty brown eyes, where emotions play,
Let resilience sparkle, let the pain fade away.

When you gaze in the Mirror, what do you see?
I see a Queen, a warrior, a strength so free.
A woman in appearance, yet a man's fortitude,
A feather-light spirit with a steel attitude.

Through late nights of toil, your strength
unwavering,
Facing the world's storms, grace never
surrenders.
In homeless shadows, you held us together,
An angel enduring, through any weather.

Options abound, yet you took the steeper route,
Through trials, you showed what courage is
about.
Unseen struggles, unknown to those who
condemn,
They can't fathom the strength that lies within.

Stop worrying, let me drape you in jewels,

Cast aside their judgments, for you're no fool.
Dream of a castle, by the serene beach,
Your sanctuary, where only joy will breach.

One day, we'll look back at how life was so
brutal,
My African Queen, no longer ruled by the cruel.
In this vision of the future, so vivid and serene,
You'll reign, my love, as an eternal African
Queen.

Haram

In the eyes of the world, they label me haram,
As if my existence is nothing but a harm.
They point their fingers,
Make me feel so small,
But do they truly understand me at all?

Haram, they say, for every choice I make,
But who are they to decide what's at stake?
My heart is pure,
My intentions are sincere,
Yet they shame me,
Spreading their fear.
They preach about sin,
About what's written clear,
But forget that forgiveness is always near.

Haram this, haram that, they never cease,
But where is the compassion, the peace?
I am more than the haram that they speak,
My faith is strong, despite the critique.

For in my heart,
I know my worth,
A precious soul, from the moment of birth.
For Islam teaches love, acceptance, and grace,

Not judgment, shame, and a constant chase.

So I rise above their words of disdain,
Embracing my faith, despite the pain.
For Allah is the judge, the ultimate guide,
And in His mercy, I will always confide.

No longer defined by the label they impose,
I find solace in His love, as it grows.
Haram, I may be, in their eyes so blind,
But in my heart, Allah's light will always shine.

Daddy's Little Girl

Daddy's little girl, a bond so sweet,
In your arms, my world is complete,
Laughter echoed in every beat,
Love entwined, a melody discreet.

Father held dreams within his gaze,
Little girl's innocence, a sunlit blaze,
Life's embrace, a tender phase
But prison bars, a cold malaise.

Daddy's little girl, a tear-stained cheek,
Memories linger, words we couldn't speak,
Visits behind bars, love's language unique,
Strength rises, each time we meet.

Father's absence, a heavy toll,
Little girl's heart, a fragile scroll,
In prison's shadow, dreams unroll,
Father, yearning, a captive soul.

Daddy's little girl, the world seems gray,
Letters penned, emotions convey,
A love resilient, come what may,
Father's spirit, a guiding ray.

Incarcerated walls, a silent scream,
Little girl's faith, a flickering beam,
In the night's hush, a whispered dream,
Father, locked away, in shadows gleams.

Daddy's little girl, resilience prevails,
Love transcends, in prison trials,
A daughter's heart, where hope sets sails,
Father's love, through justice's gales.

R&B Love

I want that R&B love,
That real love,
The kind that makes you say My, My, My
Game is so smooth that you can't help but
oblige.

There's a meeting in my bedroom tonight,
Silk sheets make me weak,
But I'm still a sista with a voice,
You ain't never met a freak like me.

If I ever fall in love again,
I'll try to not be shy,
Bumping "I Can Love You" while staring at
those pretty brown eyes.

I want to give you all of me,
But only in one condition,
Promise to not play me for a new edition.

Had my heart broken,
Never thought I'll breathe again,
It's not right but it's okay,
Cuz I learned my own strength.

Are you that somebody?
Will you be there for me?
Every day the sun won't shine,
But can you at least stay a homie?

I want that R&B love,
The one that keeps the Faith,
Soon as I get home,
You can touch me and tease me to Case.

If you had my love,
Understand that it is not ordinary,
I'll be the Bonnie to your Clyde,
Just like Jay and B in 03.

I want that R&B love,
The kind you should never take for granted,
You and are all I need to get by,
And I've realized that there is a method to all
this madness.

True love is one in a million,
And you get from it what you put in,
No playing to win,
Just that R&B love, where we both begin.